THE Archive Photographs SERIES
WATFORD

Cassiobury Park old mill.

THE
Archive Photographs
SERIES

WATFORD

Compiled by
Judith Knight

Judith Knight

CHALFORD

The Chalford Publishing Company
St Mary's Mill, Chalford,
Stroud, Gloucestershire, GL6 8NX

ISBN 0 7524 0355 9

Typesetting and origination by
The Chalford Publishing Company
Printed in Great Britain by
Redwood Books, Trowbridge

Contents

Young musicians at Clarendon School, Oxhey, 1953.

Introduction

In the period which these photographs cover, from about 1880 to 1970, the population of Watford grew from some 15,500 to nearly 80,000 people. The social, political and commercial institutions which had served the smaller town were forced to expand and become more complex. The old Local Board of Health, whose primary function was to provide a safe water supply and ensure that the town was reasonably sanitary, was succeeded by the Urban District Council, and in 1922 Borough status was achieved. The range of services provided by the Borough by the 1970s – parks, housing, arts events, leisure facilities – would have astounded the members of the original Board.

In 1880 the county directory stated that in Watford 'are corn mills, a silk factory, several malt kilns, three extensive breweries and an iron foundry. Agricultural fork handles are also made here.' By the mid-twentieth century the emphasis had changed from a semi-agricultural to an industrial climate. The largest single industry was probably printing, with ink production an important associate. Pioneering processes were developed in printing, and Odhams and the Sun Engraving Company were nationally famous. By 1970 Odhams employed 3,000 people. Engineering was another major industry, Scammell in west Watford and Rolls Royce at Leavesden being particularly important.

In the late 1990s Watford is no longer renowned for its beer, printing or engineering. To many people it is best known for its glittering shopping centre, which attracts customers from afar; the High Street has become a shadow of its former self. Yet look up above the shop entrances in the High Street, and many of the sturdy Victorian and Edwardian buildings can still be seen.

The ever changing present is often hard to cope with, and the future seems out of our control, so it is reassuring to be able to contemplate the past nostalgically through old photographs. But many changes are very much for the better: the slum courtyards have gone, the old crowded schoolrooms have been replaced by classes whose informality stimulates investigation and discovery. But no doubt the time will come when images of Watford in the 1990s will themselves be viewed with a nostalgic glow.

One
The High Street

The roundabout and pond, High Street, February 1939.

The cross roads, c.1920. Scarcely a car to be seen, only a bicycle leaning against the AA box. The Maternity and Infant Welfare Centre clinic was held in Little Nascot House on the corner of St Albans Road.

The cross roads, 1936. Major work begins on transforming the crossroads into a roundabout. The elm trees that gave their name to the house on the left were cut down.

Looking north from the pond, May 1956. The cross roads are heavily congested with traffic; this seems to be a perennial problem in the area.

The pond, 1926. The tiddlers in the pond have now been replaced by goldfish, exotic turtles and the occasional supermarket trolley.

Upton House, High Street, 1939. Upton House had been the offices of Watford Corporation and its predecessors since 1892. On the notice board the Women's Voluntary Service is asking for enrolment for ARP duties.

The fire station, High Street. Next door to the Council offices, the station was opened in June 1900, with stabling at the rear. It boasted being of 'connected to the National Telephone Company's system', and there were several street alarms in town. In the early days the firemen were volunteers although the Superintendent lived at the station.

Watford High Street, near the corner of Upton Road. The sheep are presumably on their way to be sold at Watford market, a few hundred yards to the south. Neither they, nor the shepherd, look impressed by the shop front of M Smith & Co, a 'French dyers and cleaners', established c.1902.

Watford High Street, junction of Upton Road. A snowy scene of the High Street looking north. The horses and carts seem to be making better progress than the motor car.

Golden Jubilee decorations in the High Street, 1887. At the Clarendon Road corner is a triumphal arch with Queen Victoria's portrait at the centre. Watford streets 'presented a holiday aspect such as they have never worn before'. Bells were rung, bands played, salvos were fired, and over 2,000 children assembled for tea and some well chosen words from the vicar.

Marching up the High Street, probably July 1919. This patriotic and musical procession was part of the Watford peace celebrations that ended in Cassiobury Park with such festivities as egg and spoon races and a thread the needle race for the ladies. The Empress Winter Gardens opened in 1916 and the medallions of Queen Victoria's head can just be detected at the top of the building and can still be seen today on what is now a public house.

The National Provincial Bank, High Street, c.1925. This early nineteenth-century listed building was once the premises of prominent Watford doctors Iles and Cox. Note the milestone directing travellers to Tring and Berkhamsted, and Christmas's garage with parking for sixty cars. Formerly Christmas's made and hired horse drawn vehicles.

The Market Place looking north, 1893. To welcome home the Earl of Essex and his New York bride, a replica of the Cassiobury Park gateway was erected, complete with British and American flags.

The Market Place looking north, c.1905. The Bucks and Oxon bank was taken over by Lloyds around 1902. The Corn Exchange formed part of the Essex Arms building by this date, and beyond was James Cawdell, draper and undertaker, whose department store was very well known until its demolition to make way for the new market.

Race through the Market Place, c.1904. White-aproned traders and shoppers (every one in a hat!) watch the progress of these serious looking gentlemen striding up the High Street. The front man has just passed the One Bell, King's Head and Spread Eagle public houses near the passage to the churchyard.

The Market Place, c.1902. Rogers and Gowlett, ironmongers, were the 'sole manufacturers of the Watford Wine Bin'. They also installed electric light and bells, and supplied heating apparatus for residences and greenhouses. They were on the corner of Meeting Alley, which cut through to the Baptist Chapel in Beechen Grove.

The Market Place, c.1925. This crowded scene with potential conflict between traffic, traders and pedestrians shows why the market was moved from this site. Livestock sales went to Market Street, and the stalls moved to Red Lion Yard, not far from the present undercover market.

The High Street, c.1956. Littlewoods and the Eight Bells were situated roughly where Littlewoods is today. They were both demolished in February 1956, even though the timberframed inn was of considerable architectural interest.

The Crystal Palace Beershop, 1893. A grand name for this modest building, which was situated south of the Queen's Road corner. Next door, Bishop the butcher advertises fresh pork sausages. Pearkes' business included drapery, removals, undertaking and secondhand furniture.

Fishers the butcher on the last day of trading, 1956. Above the pillars are decorative rams' heads, and bulls' heads adorn the upper windows. Francis and Percy Roads nearby are named after the sons of Frank Fisher, who was one time chairman of the Council.

Jarvis's Stores, High Street, early 1930s. The Stores, eventually taken over by Woolworths, were near the King Street corner, in a section called the People's Market, shared at various times with Mrs. Higgins Dining Rooms, an outfitter, and an eel and pie shop. What would today's Environmental Health Officers make of these open sacks and wooden boxes of loose food?

94 High Street, c.1958. The premises of the Shirt Manufacturing Company were here from 1937 to the late 1950s. Peg Brand is the name of the shirts and overalls, not the proprietor!

98 High Street. The International Stores occupied these premises just south of Church Street from 1904 until the Second War. Note the advertisement for Sylvan Glen Creamery butter, a tranquil, rural trade name.

101 High Street, 1961. Closure of the premises of Peacock's, newspaper publishers and printers, who moved to Rickmansworth Road. The firm has published the 'Watford Observer' since 1863, and was started by John Peacock in 1823.

Diamond Jubilee decorations in the High Street, 1897. The highlight of the celebrations was a procession led by 'the latest invention, a motor cycle bedecked with flowers and greenery', followed by the trades in alphabetical order – bakers, bootmen, brewers' drays, and the Volunteer Fire Brigade at the rear.

Sims, 106-8, High Street. 'Founded in 1796, this old business has been handed down in regular succession to its present proprietor, who has...an extensive and influential connection among the nobility and gentry of the district'. From a eulogy in the local directory of 1899.

High Street, 1921. Looking north, with the entrance to St Mary's churchyard left by Loosely's circulating library and stationers.

High Street, corner of King Street, c.1912. Barclay's new premises put an end to Howland's the hairdressers. On the left is the edge of the shortlived Cinema Palace, which operated from May 1911 to early 1915.

High Street, 1905. Looking south with the London and County, later Westminster Bank, on the corner of Queen's Road. H Tipple ran a butcher's shop, not a pub!

Chaters, 129 High Street, 1955. An elegant building which was listed Grade II in 1983. Jonathan Chater appeared in an 1839 directory as 'chymist and druggist and British wine dealer'. Chater's Yard, behind the shop, was redeveloped and named Albert Street in 1862.

159 High Street, c.1920. Three of the Simmons family with assistant, Harold Gorton, second left. Their trade card offered 'bobbing, shingling, waving and singeing' in the ladies' salon, with singeing and shaving for gentlemen.

159A High Street, c.1900. A grisly display of carcases outside Aubon's, at the corner of Water Lane. There are hooks for hanging meat up the outside of the shop wall.

177/179 High Street. Fred Oakley & Sons have adorned every available space with clothing, but the building's fifteenth and sixteenth century origins are still apparent.

The Lower High Street, c.1890. The projecting corn loft over the mill is a reminder of rural Watford, as is the warning notice about swine fever. The steep exterior steps were a useful precaution in an area liable to flood.

Sedgwick House and the entrance to the Brewery, Lower High Street, 1961. W F Sedgwick bought up the Watford Brewery in 1862; under Benskin's ownership it was converted to maltings. Both the handsome house and the Brewery were demolished in 1965/6.

Lower High Street, 1961. The Dumbletons were a long standing family of butchers; in 1855 James had a shop at Bushey Heath, Thomas at Clay Hill, and William at Watford. This timberframed building was demolished around 1968.

Farthing Lane, off the Lower High Street. This was court number eighteen, by Watford Field Road, and the photographer depicts a scene of 'picturesque poverty'. There are water butts, cobbled paving, strings of onions drying on the walls of seventeenth-century cottages. The two rather well turned out little girls are surely posed. On this corner was situated a Ragged School.

Jubilee decorations, Lower High Street, 1887. On the right are the West Herts Liberal Club by High Street station, with the Railway Tavern beyond. People are dressed in their best for the Queen's Golden Jubilee.

The Angel Beerhouse, Lower High Street. A late sixteenth-century brick and timber building, on the site of Ausden's yard. In 1902 a firewood dealer owned it, and it later became dining rooms.

The Wheatsheaf, Lower High Street, c.1912. This simple building, replaced in 1930, was a venue for theatrical performances early last century. Later its tea gardens were frequented by daytrippers from London, who admired the riverside scenery.

Bushey Arches, c.1870, a view through the Arches towards the Wheatsheaf. The men are leaning on the uprights of tollgates, for this was on the Sparows Herne Turnpike route that ran from Bushey to near Aylesbury. The Turnpike Trust was wound up in 1873.

Two
Around Watford

Ballards Buildings, off New Street. Women are propping up their washing with long branches in this yard, described in 1849 as one of the unhealthiest localities in the town, in which 'few dwellings have escaped the visitation of disease'.

Ballards Buildings looking towards New Street. Residents at the 1881 Census included a plasterer, pedlar, rat catcher, unemployed errand boy, lace maker, fan maker and a mill boy. The fifty five dwellings were finally demolished around 1926.

New Street, c.1956. Although very rundown here, the street was once the home of prosperous William Heydon, whose sixteenth-century chapel is in the parish church.

New Street. The entrance on the right led to Ballards Buildings. In 1881 Aaron Fisher, a cutler, and his wife Bedelia, a boot binder, kept a lodging house with thirty nine lodgers, including four Italian musicians. Nine years later the small street had a hairdresser, butcher, saddler, fishmonger as well as the lodging house.

Church Street, 1893. Old cottages in a state of dilapidation, as seen by one of Watford's greatest photographers, Frederick Downer.

King Street, 1958. The building on the right was the former Police Station of 1888. On Census night three years later the station was occupied by Superintendent Hummerstone and five prisoners, including two musicians.

Bridge Place. Formerly called Old Yard, it was described in 1849 as 'an instance of the injurious effect of an open cesspool'. Sixty-two people inhabited fifteen cottages, and rents decreased with proximity to the cesspool.

William Coles' studio at 60 Queen's Road, c.1890. These were the first premises of another of Watford's great photographers who died aged eighty-four in 1938. Grevilles took the business over in 1928.

The former Fighting Cocks Inn, Water Lane, 1910. Nineteenth-century Watford historian Henry Williams says that boats could be hired from here to row up the Colne to Bushey Mill Bridge.

Market Street, 1926. A temporary bus stop to Garston and beyond, situated near the corner of the street where the present Post Office stands.

The Morrison Almshouses, Vicarage Road, 1961. These were built in 1824, though the original charity of Dame Dorothy Morrison was founded in 1613. They were demolished in the mid 1960s.

The Bedford Almshouses, Church Street, c.1955. Founded for eight poor women in 1580 by Frances, Earl of Bedford, and his wife Bridget, these are Watford's oldest dwellings. They were restored in 1959.

George Ausden's delivery van, c.1911. The workforce of the long established firm of Ausden's are posing in Market Street.

Albert Street, 1934. The rear of the street showing the wash houses on the left. The suspicious looking characters are probably from the Borough Council! The street was demolished in the early 1960s.

Beechen Grove Baptist church, c.1888. The church itself was completed in October 1878, but the photograph probably shows the laying of the foundation stone of the lecture hall which opened in 1888.

Cassio Hamlet, Hempstead Road. Haycarts passing the Horns Public House on their way to the High Street.

St Albans Road. The large house, Little Nascot, was the home from 1842 of C.F. Humbert of the surveying firm Humbert and Flint. In its latter years it housed the child guidance clinic, and was demolished in 1959.

24-38 St Albans Road, September 1965. Houses in the French Second Empire style between St John's and Wellington roads.

Bridge on Balmoral Road, 1956. The notice board includes an advertisement for Sir Adrian Boult performing at the Town Hall.

The Hare Public House in Leavesden High Road, 1950. This modest pub was demolished in 1958, and a new one now occupies the site.

Watford Fields, 1957. The houses were built before car ownership, with the need for garages, was common. Or are these car owners visiting the Cricketers Beer House on the left?

Ashwell's Yard, early 1920s. The courtyard led off the High Street, near present day Charter Place.

Three

People at Work

St Albans Road Field on Bushey Lodge Farm, 1918. A rural scene taken from the balcony of a house in Bushey Mill Lane. Soldiers are working under the direction of the farmer.

Reaping, with the Caledonian Schools in the background. The Royal Caledonian Schools were founded as a memorial to the Scottish soldiers at Waterloo, and moved to Bushey in 1903.

Callowland Farm. The farm was off Leavesden Road, south of Gammons lane. The men do not seem to be in normal working attire!

CALLOW LAND FARM, WATFORD.

The last of Harwoods Farm, 1957. The premises of Hempsall, undertakers, in one of the remaining outbuildings of the farm. The name 'Harwood' occurs in the early sixteenth century, and the estate was still farmed until c.1900.

Grove Mill Lane. 'Grove Mill, a remarkably pleasant situation', wrote John Hassell in 1819, but the mill in this photograph was not built until around 1875. A hundred years later it was converted into apartments.

The Grand Union Canal frozen over, c.1900. Taken from a lantern slide by Frederick Downer, this shows the canal folk in traditional costume.

Fire escape drill. Watford Fire Brigade practising their skills, with time to pose for Downer's camera. The role of the dog is unclear.

Sedgwick's Brewery, c.1964. Long since taken over by nearby Benskin's, and used as a maltings, most of the remaining Sedgwick buildings were demolished in 1965/6.

Cassiobury Saw Mills. Thomas Turner's saw mills adjoined the Junction station off the St Albans Road, on the site later occupied by Fishburn's. The firm produced a variety of wooden and metal goods, including fencing, clothes horses, sheep troughs, gymnastic apparatus and 'the celebrated Cassiobury croquet' equipment. It is not known what event is being celebrated in the photograph. The children look very well dressed; some are even wearing fur tippets.

Watford Mill, Lower High Street, 1924/5. The sad exterior of the former flour mill whose premises were gutted by fire in December 1924.

Rogers' timberyard, 1921. The charred remains of part of the premises of Walter Rogers, coal and timber merchants, behind the High Street between Beechen Grove and Meetings Alley. Ironically the firm was agent for a major fire insurance company.

The Watford Bypass, August 1928. The early days of NorthWestern Avenue, looking towards Watford. The horsedrawn vehicle contrasts with the invitation to fill up with Pratt's petrol.

Building the pedestrian underpass, February 1972. A view from Hempstead Road, showing part of the new central area redevelopment.

Widening the Hempstead Road. One of the reconstructions of the Hempstead Road, c.1950.

Construction of the reservoir at Bushey Heath, 1898. Manual and horse power combine in a period unaffected by health and safety regulations. The surveyor is clearly a 'gentleman'.

Sequah's meeting, June 1890. Born in Cornwall under a more prosaic name, Sequah claimed to be an American 'medicine man', who could cure all ills with his bottled remedy. He performed from a gilt carriage with musical accompaniment, and all Watford's great and good, including the Earl of Essex, patronised his farewell concert.

Metropolitan Railway bus, October 1928. The buses ran from the Met. station to St Mary's church. This one is promoting Watford's Shopping Week.

Opening of the Metropolitan Railway station, 2 November 1925. The local paper was sceptical about the cost effectiveness of the new line, and how long before it paid for itself: 'Although only two and a half miles, well over a quarter of a million being spent on it'.

General Strike, 12 May 1926. The Market place on the final day of the strike. The production of the 'Watford Observer' was disrupted, and a bus window broken, but no significant events occurred in Watford.

A Watford posting station, early 1900s. Downer captured this eye catching mixture of local and national advertisements.

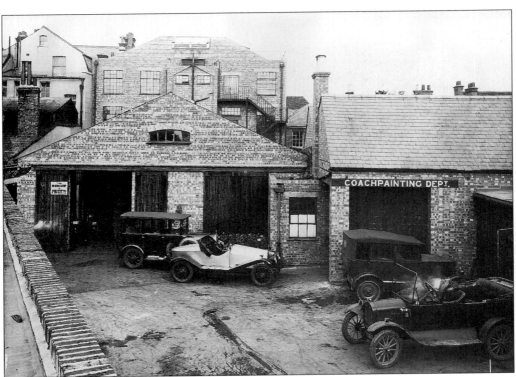

Rear of 54-56 High Street. The workshop of A. Christmas and Co. whose adaptability helped them prosper during the changeover from the horsedrawn to the horseless carriage.

George Ausden's van parked in the Rose and Crown Yard, c.1919.

Accident in the High Street. A disastrous end to a steam roller near the Queen's Road corner.

The Fire Brigade, 1899. The newly formed Watford Local Board Fire Brigade; on their badges are the letters WLB.

Fire at Morrison Jones and Co.'s cabinet factory at the Rookery, 17 August 1910. It took over five hours of the combined efforts of three Fire Brigades from Watford, Sedgwick's Brewery and Rickmansworth to extinguish this fire. After the collapse of the clock tower five brave men fought the blaze from within the building.

Colin Taylor, coal and corn merchant. The staff, photographed by Coles, in carnival mood, many wearing their Oddfellows sashes. The float shows a large piece of coal, proudly stating 'No dust'.

Whippendell Woods wardens, 1935. The parks superintendent holding the first meeting with his voluntary wardens who included Scout masters and members of the Watford Amenities Preservation Society.

The Post Office in Queen's Road. Built in 1886 by the Derby Road corner on the site of a previous temporary building, the Post Office was demolished in 1978.

The Post Office staff, c.1890. The staff are wearing their employee number on their collars. The Postmaster, J. H. Morley is seated in the centre.

Four
Education and Welfare

The Watford Endowed School, Derby Road. Built by Thomas Turner of Cassiobury Saw Mills, the premises opened in April 1884, in place of the old Free School building which was now much too small.

The staff of the Endowed School for Boys. The first headmaster of what was to become the Grammar School was W. R. Carter, seated centre. He remained head until the school moved once more to its present site in Rickmansworth Road.

The Free School. The School was built in 1704, by the generosity of Elizabeth Fuller, to educate poor children in Watford. The handsome building still stands 'adjoyning the churchyard'.

The Church Street National School. The school opened in 1841, and after closure in 1922 the building served other purposes, including Register Office. The presence of the cars is a sad reminder that a multi storey car park now occupies the site.

Miss Diggle's school in Queen's Road. The 1871 Census lists Fanny Diggle, schoolmistress aged twenty-seven, born in Bolton. Her pupils look distinctly cheerless, despite the likelihood of a game of croquet.

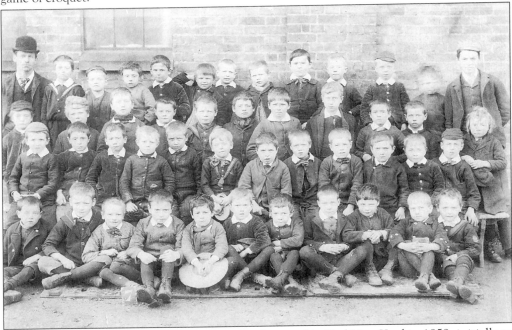

Beechen Grove Board School, 1892. The school opened in Red Lion Yard in 1859, initially to provide nonconformist instruction to forty boys and 110 girls. It transferred to the Local School Board in 1883.

The Caledonian Schools, Bushey, 1928.
The Duke and Duchess of Atholl visited
the school on 14 July for prizegiving and
the opening of extensions to the building.

The Caledonian School, Bushey, 1928. The staff with the Duke and Duchess in the front row.

Callowland Girls' School, 1903. The girls' and infants' schools opened in 1892, and the boys' section a year later. In recent years the buildings have been an adult education centre.

Leavesden Green J.M.I., a postwar prefabricated building. A notice on the board displays the name of today's floortidying monitor and classroom messenger. In all respects this scene contrasts with formality of the earlier school photographs.

The London Orphan Asylum. A charitable foundation, the school moved from London to Watford in 1871. It was intended for 'respectable fatherless boys and girls from every part of the United Kingdom'.

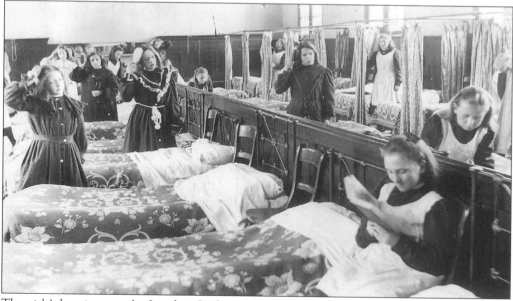

The girls' dormitory at the London Orphan Asylum. Early morning hairbrushing duty. School rules were rigid but by no means unkind.

St John's Ambulance Brigade, 1905. Stretcher bearers at attention in the fields to the south of St Mary's church.

The staff of the Isolation Hospital, c.1922. The hospital, sited off Tolpits Lane, was built in 1895. In the year of this photograph 161 patients were admitted, mainly with scarlet fever and diphtheria.

The Peace Memorial Hospital, c.1926. The hospital was opened by the Princess Royal in 1925, paid for largely by public subscription. The large balconies were for open air treatment.

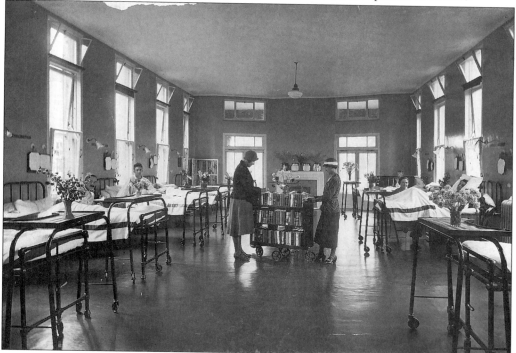

The hospital library service. Volunteers at the Peace Memorial Hospital dispensing books to the patients.

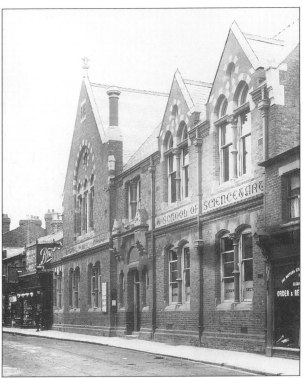

Watford Public Library, Queen's Road. The library opened in 1874 and was soon enlarged to house the School of Science, Art and Literature and the School of Music. Subjects taught ranged from building construction to shorthand, and university extension courses were also on offer.

Interior of Watford Public Library, Queen's Road. When the new library was opened on its present site in 1928, this building continued to be used for education.

Watford Central Library, 1928. A contemporary architectural journal stated that the new library 'has the quiet charm of good fenestration and dignified proportions'. Originally only the lecture hall was upstairs.

Cleaning the books in the Central Library, c.1930. Some progress has been made over the last sixty years!

Watford Technical College, c.1955. The college's official opening was on 15 May 1953, though the ground floor had been built before the war. Its six departments were Art, Building, Commerce, Printing, Technology and Domestic Science.

Concert by Watford School of Music, 1905. Staff and students performing at the Clarendon Hall under the baton of E. Howard Jones, professor at the Royal Academy of Music. It is probable that this is their performance of Mendelssohn's 'Elijah'.

Five

War and Peace

Bandsmen of the Hertfordshire Rifle Volunteers. Young musicians in plumed shakos and frogged tunics, possibly from the Second Hertfordshire (Watford) Rifle Volunteers.

Troops in the High Street, 1900. The 42nd (Hertfordshire) Company, Imperial Yeomanry trained in Watford before embarking for South Africa.

More Boer War troops in the High Street, 1900. A photograph by Downer of officers and men from the same Company of mounted infantry.

Probably the 'sendoff' held on 3 March 1900 for the men setting off for the front.

Soldiers marching through Watford during the First World War.

The local Volunteer band attend a funeral in The Avenue, during the First World War.

Special Constables in the High Street, 1916. Wearing white 'on duty' armbands, the Specials parade past the Pond.

Parade leaving the Clarendon Drill Hall, March 1929. British Legion veterans and civic officials march from the Hall to St Mary's church.

The British Legion Headquarters, 1919. The opening of the Comrades of the Great War club house at 12 St Albans Road.

Armistice Day service, 1924. Two minutes silence ouside the Council offices in Upton Road, against a curiously inappropriate background of advertisements.

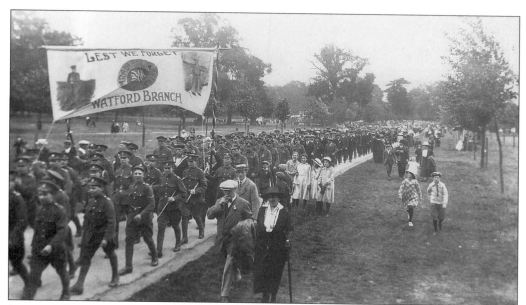

Peace celebrations in Cassiobury Park, 19 July 1919. All ex-Servicemen were invited to join in the procession from the Market Place to the Park where the Last Post was sounded. Afterwards entertainment included music, dancing and races and a tug-of-war between Fishers the butchers and M.A. Sedgwick's.

War memorial outside the Peace Memorial Hospital. Sculpted by Mary Bromet, the 'spirit of war' group was unveiled in July 1928. It was later moved to a site beside the Town Hall.

Air Defence Cadet Corps being inspected, 1939.

Children's first aid party, October 1941. Serious fun with a smiling patient. Note the F.A.P. on the berets.

The Home Guard, August 1941. Anti-tank training for the Hertfordshire Home Guards during a weekend course at Russells in the Hempstead Road.

Sandbagging the Peace Memorial Hospital, August 1939. Air raid precautions the week before the outbreak of war.

Bomb damage to St John's Road, 5 December 1940. The Civil Defence bulletin reported 'At 20.18 hours an H.E. bomb fell on and demolished two houses, 19 and 20 St John's Road. Five persons were killed and one injured...'.

Bomb damage at Trewins, January 1941. In the early hours of the morning of 2 January, a number of incendiary bombs fell on the Queen's Road area, causing a serious fire in Trewins store.

Watford readers are encouraged to donate their books as part of the salvage drive, 1942-3.

The British Restaurant at Alpha House in St Albans Road. Having opened the restaurant, the mayor and mayoress bought Monday's lunch: tomato soup, beef with mashed potatoes, carrots, bread, and date pudding with custard. Cost? One shilling.

Watford schoolchildren await children from Mainz on the Met. station, 1963. The link between the two towns, both famous for printing, was forged in 1956, and regular contact is made between them.

Six

Sport and Leisure

The West Herts Whitsuntide athletic sports meeting, 27 May 1893.

The cycling races occupied much of the programme, and 'the gate was the largest ever known' at the West Herts sports ground. The Earl of Essex, president of the Club and the ground, presented the prizes.

The Watford Cycling Club, c.1902.

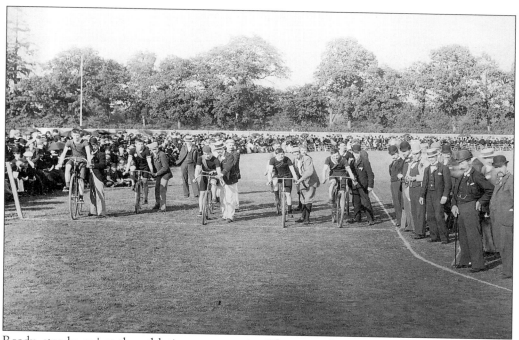

Ready, steady, go! at the athletic sports meeting. The start of one of the bicycle races, perhaps the 880-yard or the one-mile handicap. Prizes for these were a silvermounted dressing bag and a silver jug.

The West Herts athletic sports meeting again. The Earl of Essex, (on the pavilion next to the small boy in the boater), said that sport always would be 'one of the greatest characteristics of all Englishmen.'

School sports day, 1920. Proud relations at a sports day held on the West Herts ground. The shield was presented by R. A. Thorpe, later a mayor of Watford.

Tug-of-war, West Herts sports ground, May 1893. Members of Watford Local Board versus Croxley Paper Mills. The Watford officials won.

Tennis match on the West Herts sports ground, 1910. One of the ladies in the background is playing in a large hat!

The Upton Road Bowling Club, c.1920. The club existed from the beginning of the First World War until the mid 1920s.

Bowls match in Cassiobury Park, c.1934. Players from Bushey Grove, North Watford, Kings Langley and the Ovaltine Clubs in a representative match. Greenkeeper W. Tillyard is centre of the back row.

The Gentlemen of Herts v. West Herts, 19 and 20 July 1897. It is not surprising that the Gentlemen were 'dismissed', since West Herts had the great batsman Prince Ranjitsinhji in their side. He made 161 runs!

Opening of the Woodside Sports Arena, 4 November 1955. The Duke of Edinburgh with the mayor, Alderman Edward Amey. After the ceremony a relay of runners conveyed a loyal greeting for the Queen from the Town Hall to the arena.

The King's Head, Hunton Bridge. This photograph is annotated 'after the alterations', and all the staff have turned out to have their picture taken outside the refurbished premises.

The Essex Arms Hotel, 1901. An important inn for over a century, the Essex Arms was demolished when Cawdells drapery business was extended.

The Rose and Crown. This major coaching inn was on the corner of Market Street and was rebuilt several times.

The Dog, Hempstead Road, 1931. A modest pub, much used by hay carters, which was demolished in 1969. There is a pigeon loft in the outhouse.

The Badminton Banjo Team entertaining at the Coronation celebrations in Cassiobury Park, 1902. Among the songs performed were 'Tell me, honey, do', 'The bounder' and 'The lay of the very last minstrel'.

Watford Horse Show. Hunters being judged on the Vicarage Road football ground.

Bridge in Cassiobury Park. The River Gade with five symmetrically posed youngsters.

Locks over the Grand Union Canal, 1955. A working boat is manoeuvred through the locks in Cassiobury Park.

The Diamond Jubilee bonfire, 1897. The celebrations in Watford exceeded those for the Golden Jubilee. This giant bonfire was built on Harwoods Farm where a grand firework display was held. The Council officials look rather incongruous in front of it!

Seven

People and Places

Floods in Lower High Street, 16 June 1903. Fifty-nine hours of rain led to a flood from the Five Arches, across Benskin's cricket ground up as far as the gas works. There was reported to be 'more water than beer' in the Hit and Miss pub!

Floods, March 1947. Gallant behaviour as flood water makes Walton Road impassable.

Floods, March 1947, showing the advantages of horsedrawn transport.

The milk delivery gets through,
March or April 1947.

Westminster Bank, High Street. The facade of this handsome neo-classical building dating from 1931 has been retained, but it is now a public house.

The Labour church, Durban Road, c.1901. The building, decorated with Walter Crane drawings, was erected in 1901. Its doctrine was unconventional – a kind of Christian Socialism without much religion. The banner above the stage reads 'Workers of the world, unite'.

The Limes, St Albans Road. The house, described in a 1912 sales catalogue as a 'charming, old fashioned, ivy-clad residence', was just north of the High Street corner.

The Grove, c.1980. Built in 1756 for Thomas Villiers, later the Earl of Clarendon, the Grove has served at various times as a fashionable home, an hotel, a school, a wartime railway HQ, and a management college.

The Elms, High Street, c.1930. During the 1920s this handsome early eighteenth-century house became a residential hotel. It was demolished to make way for the Town Hall.

The interior of Garston Manor. The house, in High Elms Lane, was built around 1841. When the estate was sold off in 1932 the house boasted a ballroom, billiard room, drawing room, library, thirteen main bedrooms, with ten more for staff, and an extensive cellarage.

Woodside House, 1950s. The house was demolished in 1959.

The Clarendon Hotel, Station Road, 1966. The hotel looks very much as it did in a print of 1862 shortly after it was built. Renamed Benskin House, it became the brewers' offices, and is now a solicitors.

The last of Wiggen Hall, 1959. It was once the home of the Deacon family, whose name is remembered in nearby Deacon's Hill.

Langleybury, c.1900. The house was completed in 1729 for Sir Robert Raymond, first Baron of Abbots Langley. More recently it has served as the library for Langleybury School.

Holywell House, 1958. The Council owned the house and the farm became part of the sewage works. Holywell Estate is now on the site.

Cassiobury House. Watford's most famous house, seat of the Earls of Essex. Sold in 1922, it was demolished in 1927.

The orangery at Cassiobury House. A garden party at Cassiobury in its heyday, with Lady Essex and some Watford dignitaries.

Entrance lodge to Cassiobury Park, Rickmansworth Road, 1959. The demolition in 1970 of the lodge and gates has never been forgotten or forgiven by Watfordians.

Little Cassiobury, Hempstead Road, c.1900. Described by Pevsner as 'the best classical house in Watford', it was built in the late seventeenth century as the Dower House. It is now occupied by the County Council.

Oxhey chapel before 1897. The chapel was built in 1612 for the judge Sir James Altham, whose monument is within. Its surroundings are now more urban!

Holy Rood church, Market Street, c.1895. The observant will spot that the tower of this fine gothic revival church is not yet built. The architect was J. F. Bentley, later the architect of Westminster Cathedral.

The Lecturer's House, October 1965. The residence, near St Mary's church, of the 'Lecturer', supported from 1613 by Lady Elizabeth Russell. His duties were to deliver a weekly lecture or sermon.

St Mary's church in quieter times. Watford's fine parish church, with a thirteenth-century chancel, is now largely hidden from the High Street. The Morrison chapel has outstanding monuments to the early owners of Cassiobury.

The West Herts Liberal Club, High Street. The club's headquarters adjoined the High Street station.

The Conservative Club, 31 High Street. It was situated on the southern corner of Clarendon Road next door to the Lime Tree Temperance Hotel.

Charter Day, 18 October 1922. The mayor, Lord Clarendon, is presented with the Borough Charter at Haydon Road which marks the boundary between Watford and Bushey. A procession followed this ceremony, and the Proclamation of the Charter was read from the Essex Arms.

Watford Borough Council members and officers, 1931.

Officers and civic dignitaries. Some notables are the Reverend Lee James, seated with a shawl, and on his left E. J. Slinn, Chairman of the Council. The Town Clerk, Henry Morten Turner, stands fourth from left.

Opening of the new market, 25 September 1928. Alderman Rushton is presented with a symbolic basket of produce. The stallholders lamented leaving the traditional site in Market Place, but conceded that electricity might have some advantages. Work began on covering the market in 1932.

Watford Market, September 1950. While Charter Place was being built, the market had to move to temporary premises in Shrubbery car park.

The seventh Earl of Essex, December 1893. A portrait taken on his marriage to Adele Grant. In his speech to the people of Watford he spoke of the 'fellowship and sympathy between the owners of Cassiobury and the inhabitants of Watford'.

The sixth Earl and the Countess of Clarendon before 1922. The Earl, Charter Mayor of Watford in 1922, was chairman of the BBC in the late 1920s, and later the Governor of South Africa.

Arthur, sixth Earl of Essex. A Downer cabinet portrait of the Earl in velvet walking attire. He died in 1892 in his ninetieth year.

Studio portrait of Lady Essex, wife of the sixth Earl.

Mr and Mrs Frederick Thomas Trewin. He was a veterinary surgeon who originally practised in Queen's Road next door to the family drapery business, and later had premises on the corner of Clarendon Road and the High Street.

The Ayres family. C.P.Ayres was an architect and onetime chairman of the Urban District Council. His daughter Ruby became a best selling romantic novelist.

Frederick Downer and family, late 1890s. Frederick, shown seated in the middle, photographed people and places widely, and also used to hold lantern slide shows. He died in 1919.

The staff of Victoria School, 1909-10. The school, opened in January 1898, was in Addiscombe Road.

Dr Brett. Not only was Dr Brett the first Medical Officer of Health for Watford U.D., but he also promoted the library, education, street improvements, and the good of the community generally. He died in 1896.

Declaration of the General Election results, 8 December 1910. Arnold Ward, Conservative MP for West Herts, was re-elected. His Liberal opponent had been vigorously supported by Suffragettes.

Sergeant Major Maxted, the first macebearer of the newly formed Borough of Watford, 1922.

'The old gardener on the estate, top of King Street'. Can anyone identify him?

Richard André, c.1910. A flamboyant author and illustrator, and pioneer of colour process engraving, he was one of the founders of the firm of André and Sleigh of Bushey, that much later became the Sun Engraving Co.

J. P. Taylor, c.1900. The founder of the High Street firm of tailors with the tools of his craft. In 1908 he advertised 'Riding breeches a speciality. Motor clothing in every quality and description'.

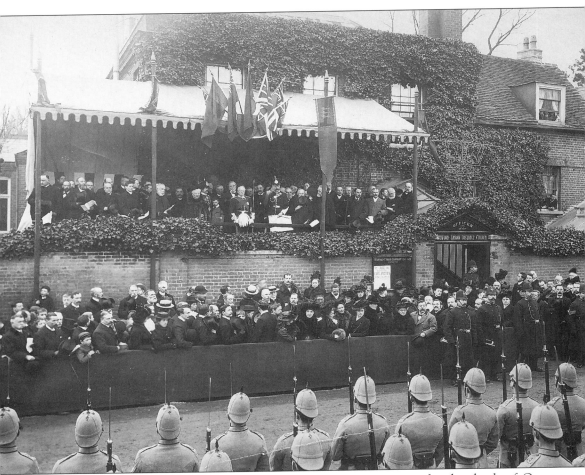

Proclamation of Edward VII, January 1901. A scene of mourning for the death of Queen Victoria. King Edward's coronation did not take place until August 1902, delayed for some weeks by the King's ill health. Disappointment at the delay of the celebrations led to rioting in Watford.

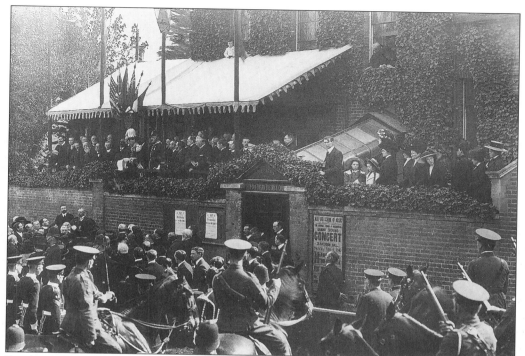

Proclamation of King George V, 12 May 1910. A new King proclaimed but 'a stupendous blow had fallen upon the nation and nowhere was the stunning force of its staggering weight felt more heavily than in Watford.'

Celebrations and splendid hats in Cassiobury Park for the coronation of George V.

Rigby Taylor presenting a sports shield to Chater school. Taylor was deputy mayor, and chairman of Watford Football Club in 1939.

Market day in the High Street.

Band of Hope rally, c.1905. The banners show representatives from many different nonconformist churches. George Longley, draper and well-known Watford personality, leads.

The Palace Theatre, 1922. The foundation stone of Watford's theatre was laid in June 1908 and the curtain went up six months later on a variety programme. Famous names from Harry Lauder to Donald Wolfit have trodden its boards, and the theatre has an excellent reputation nationally.

Hempstead Road Baths. When the baths opened on 10 May 1933 they were believed to be the first all-electric baths in the world. The chairman of the baths Committee declared 'May these baths still be going strong in 2033!'

Watford Central Library around 1950.

Acknowledgements

All the photographs in the book are held in the local collection at Watford Central Library and apologies are offered to anyone whose material has inadvertently been used without due acknowledgement. Kelly's and Peacock's street directories and the files of the local newspapers have provided invaluable background information. Thanks are due to colleagues at the library who have been patient while the book was being compiled.

Stock List

(Titles are listed according to the pre-1974 county boundaries)

BERKSHIRE

Wantage
Irene Hancock
ISBN 0-7524-0146 7

CARDIGANSHIRE

Aberaeron and Mid Ceredigion
William Howells
ISBN 0-7524-0106-8

CHESHIRE

Ashton-under-Lyne and Mossley
Alice Lock
ISBN 0-7524-0164-5

Around Bebington
Pat O'Brien
ISBN 0-7524-0121-1

Crewe
Brian Edge
ISBN 0-7524-0052-5

Frodsham and Helsby
Frodsham and District Local History Group
ISBN 0-7524-0161-0

Macclesfield Silk
Moira Stevenson and Louanne Collins
ISBN 0-7524-0315 X

Marple
Steve Cliffe
ISBN 0-7524-0316-8

Runcorn
Bert Starkey
ISBN 0-7524-0025-8

Warrington
Janice Hayes
ISBN 0-7524-0040-1

West Kirby to Hoylake
Jim O'Neil
ISBN 0-7524-0024-X

Widnes
Anne Hall and the Widnes Historical Society
ISBN 0-7524-0117-3

CORNWALL

Padstow
Malcolm McCarthy
ISBN 0-7524-0033-9

St Ives Bay
Jonathan Holmes
ISBN 0-7524-0186-6

COUNTY DURHAM

Bishop Auckland
John Land
ISBN 0-7524-0312-5

Around Shildon
Vera Chapman
ISBN 0-7524-0115-7

CUMBERLAND

Carlisle
Dennis Perriam
ISBN 0-7524-0166-1

DERBYSHIRE

Around Alfreton
Alfreton and District Heritage Trust
ISBN 0-7524-0041-X

Barlborough, Clowne, Creswell and Whitwell
Les Yaw
ISBN 0-7524-0031-2

Around Bolsover
Bernard Haigh
ISBN 0-7524-0021-5

Around Derby
Alan Champion and Mark Edworthy
ISBN 0-7524-0020-7

Long Eaton
John Barker
ISBN 0-7524-0110-6

Ripley and Codnor
David Buxton
ISBN 0-7524-0042-8

Shirebrook
Geoff Sadler
ISBN 0-7524-0028-2

Shirebrook: A Second Selection
Geoff Sadler
ISBN 0-7524-0317-6

DEVON

Brixham
Ted Gosling and Lyn Marshall
ISBN 0-7524-0037-1

Around Honiton
Les Berry and Gerald Gosling
ISBN 0-7524-0175-0

Around Newton Abbot
Les Berry and Gerald Gosling
ISBN 0-7524-0027-4

Around Ottery St Mary
Gerald Gosling and Peter Harris
ISBN 0-7524-0030-4

Around Sidmouth
Les Berry and Gerald Gosling
ISBN 0-7524-0137-8

DORSET

Around Uplyme and Lyme Regis
Les Berry and Gerald Gosling
ISBN 0-7524-0044-4

ESSEX

Braintree and Bocking
John and Sandra Adlam and Mark Charlton
ISBN 0-7524-0129-7

Ilford
Ian Dowling and Nick Harris
ISBN 0-7524-0050-9

Ilford: A Second Selection
Ian Dowling and Nick Harris
ISBN 0-7524-0320-6

Saffron Walden
Jean Gumbrell
ISBN 0-7524-0176-9

GLAMORGAN

Around Bridgend
Simon Eckley
ISBN 0-7524-0189-0

Caerphilly
Simon Eckley
ISBN 0-7524-0194-7

Around Kenfig Hill and Pyle
Keith Morgan
ISBN 0-7524-0314-1

The County Borough of Merthyr Tydfil
Carolyn Jacob, Stephen Done and Simon Eckley
ISBN 0-7524-0012-6

Mountain Ash, Penrhiwceiber and Abercynon
Bernard Baldwin and Harry Rogers
ISBN 0-7524-0114-9

Pontypridd
Simon Eckley
ISBN 0-7524-0017-7

Rhondda
Simon Eckley and Emrys Jenkins
ISBN 0-7524-0028-2

Rhondda: A Second Selection
Simon Eckley and Emrys Jenkins
ISBN 0-7524-0308-7

Roath, Splott, and Adamsdown
Roath Local History Society
ISBN 0-7524-0199-8

GLOUCESTERSHIRE

Barnwood, Hucclecote and Brockworth
Alan Sutton
ISBN 0-7524-0000-2

Forest to Severn
Humphrey Phelps
ISBN 0-7524-0008-8

Filton and the Flying Machine
Malcolm Hall
ISBN 0-7524-0171-8

Gloster Aircraft Company
Derek James
ISBN 0-7524-0038-X

The City of Gloucester
Jill Voyce
ISBN 0-7524-0306-0

Around Nailsworth and Minchinhampton from the Conway Collection
Howard Beard
ISBN 0-7524-0048-7

Around Newent
Tim Ward
ISBN 0-7524-0003-7

Stroud: Five Stroud Photographers
Howard Beard, Peter Harris and Wilf Merrett
ISBN 0-7524-0305-2

HAMPSHIRE

Gosport
Ian Edelman
ISBN 0-7524-0300-1

Winchester from the Sollars Collection
John Brimfield
ISBN 0-7524-0173-4

HEREFORDSHIRE

Ross-on-Wye
Tom Rigby and Alan Sutton
ISBN 0-7524-0002-9

HERTFORDSHIRE

Buntingford
Philip Plumb
ISBN 0-7524-0170-X

Hampstead Garden Suburb
Mervyn Miller
ISBN 0-7524-0319-2

Hemel Hempstead
Eve Davis
ISBN 0-7524-0167-X

Letchworth
Mervyn Miller
ISBN 0-7524-0318-4

Welwyn Garden City
Angela Eserin
ISBN 0-7524-0133-5

KENT

Hythe
Joy Melville and Angela Lewis-Johnson
ISBN 0-7524-0169-6

North Thanet Coast
Alan Kay
ISBN 0-7524-0112-2

Shorts Aircraft
Mike Hooks
ISBN 0-7524-0193-9

LANCASHIRE

Lancaster and the Lune Valley
Robert Alston
ISBN 0-7524-0015-0

Morecambe Bay
Robert Alston
ISBN 0-7524-0163-7

Manchester
Peter Stewart
ISBN 0-7524-0103-3

LINCOLNSHIRE

Louth
David Cuppleditch
ISBN 0-7524-0172-6

Stamford
David Gerard
ISBN 0-7524-0309-5

LONDON
(Greater London and Middlesex)

Battersea and Clapham
Patrick Loobey
ISBN 0-7524-0010-X

Canning Town
Howard Bloch and Nick Harris
ISBN 0-7524-0057-6

Chiswick
Carolyn and Peter Hammond
ISBN 0-7524-0001-0

Forest Gate
Nick Harris and Dorcas Sanders
ISBN 0-7524-0049-5

Greenwich
Barbara Ludlow
ISBN 0-7524-0045-2

Highgate and Muswell Hill
Joan Schwitzer and Ken Gay
ISBN 0-7524-0119-X

Islington
Gavin Smith
ISBN 0-7524-0140-8

Lewisham
John Coulter and Barry Olley
ISBN 0-7524-0059-2

Leyton and Leytonstone
Keith Romig and Peter Lawrence
ISBN 0-7524-0158-0

Newham Dockland
Howard Bloch
ISBN 0-7524-0107-6

Norwood
Nicholas Reed
ISBN 0-7524-0147-5

Peckham and Nunhead
John D. Beasley
ISBN 0-7524-0122-X

Piccadilly Circus
David Oxford
ISBN 0-7524-0196-3

Stoke Newington
Gavin Smith
ISBN 0-7524-0159-9

Sydenham and Forest Hill
John Coulter and John Seaman
ISBN 0-7524-0036-3

Wandsworth
Patrick Loobey
ISBN 0-7524-0026-6

Wanstead and Woodford
Ian Dowling and Nick Harris
ISBN 0-7524-0113-0

MONMOUTHSHIRE

Vanished Abergavenny
Frank Olding
ISBN 0-7524-0034-7

Abertillery, Aberbeeg and Llanhilleth
*Abertillery and District Museum Society and Simon
Eckley*
ISBN 0-7524-0134-3

Blaina, Nantyglo and Brynmawr
Trevor Rowson
ISBN 0-7524-0136-X

NORFOLK

North Norfolk
Cliff Richard Temple
ISBN 0-7524-0149-1

NOTTINGHAMSHIRE

Nottingham 1897–1947
Douglas Whitworth
ISBN 0-7524-0157-2

OXFORDSHIRE

Banbury
Tom Rigby
ISBN 0-7524-0013-4

PEMBROKESHIRE

Saundersfoot and Tenby
Ken Daniels
ISBN 0-7524-0192-0

RADNORSHIRE

Llandrindod Wells
Chris Wilson
ISBN 0-7524-0191-2

SHROPSHIRE

Leominster
Eric Turton
ISBN 0-7524-0307-9

Ludlow
David Lloyd
ISBN 0-7524-0155-6

Oswestry
Bernard Mitchell
ISBN 0-7524-0032-0

**North Telford: Wellington, Oakengates, and
Surrounding Areas**
John Powell and Michael A. Vanns
ISBN 0-7524-0124-6

**South Telford: Ironbridge Gorge, Madeley, and
Dawley**
John Powell and Michael A. Vanns
ISBN 0-7524-0125-4

SOMERSET

Bath
Paul De'Ath
ISBN 0-7524-0127-0

Around Yeovil
Robin Ansell and Marion Barnes
ISBN 0-7524-0178-5

STAFFORDSHIRE

Cannock Chase
Sherry Belcher and Mary Mills
ISBN 0-7524-0051-7

Around Cheadle
George Short
ISBN 0-7524-0022-3

The Potteries
Ian Lawley
ISBN 0-7524-0046-0

East Staffordshire
Geoffrey Sowerby and Richard Farman
ISBN 0-7524-0197-1

SUFFOLK

Lowestoft to Southwold
Humphrey Phelps
ISBN 0-7524-0108-4

Walberswick to Felixstowe
Humphrey Phelps
ISBN 0-7524-0109-2

SURREY

Around Camberley
Ken Clarke
ISBN 0-7524-0148-3

Around Cranleigh
Michael Miller
ISBN 0-7524-0143-2

Epsom and Ewell
Richard Essen
ISBN 0-7524-0111-4

Farnham by the Wey
Jean Parratt
ISBN 0-7524-0185-8

Industrious Surrey: Historic Images of the County at Work
Chris Shepheard
ISBN 0-7524-0009-6

Reigate and Redhill
Mary G. Goss
ISBN 0-7524-0179-3

Richmond and Kew
Richard Essen
ISBN 0-7524-0145-9

SUSSEX

Billingshurst
Wendy Lines
ISBN 0-7524-0301-X

WARWICKSHIRE

Central Birmingham 1870–1920
Keith Turner
ISBN 0-7524-0053-3

Old Harborne
Roy Clarke
ISBN 0-7524-0054-1

WILTSHIRE

Malmesbury
Dorothy Barnes
ISBN 0-7524-0177-7

Great Western Swindon
Tim Bryan
ISBN 0-7524-0153-X

Midland and South Western Junction Railway
Mike Barnsley and Brian Bridgeman
ISBN 0-7524-0016-9

WORCESTERSHIRE

Around Malvern
Keith Smith
ISBN 0-7524-0029-0

YORKSHIRE
(EAST RIDING)

Hornsea
G.L. Southwell
ISBN 0-7524-0120-3

YORKSHIRE
(NORTH RIDING)

Northallerton
Vera Chapman
ISBN 0-7524-055-X

Scarborough in the 1970s and 1980s
Richard Percy
ISBN 0-7524-0325-7

YORKSHIRE
(WEST RIDING)

Barnsley
Barnsley Archive Service
ISBN 0-7524-0188-2

Bingley
Bingley and District Local History Society
ISBN 0-7524-0311-7

Bradford
Gary Firth
ISBN 0-7524-0313-3

Castleford
Wakefield Metropolitan District Council
ISBN 0-7524-0047-9

Doncaster
Peter Tuffrey
ISBN 0-7524-0162-9

Harrogate
Malcolm Neesam
ISBN 0-7524-0154-8

Holme Valley
Peter and Iris Bullock
ISBN 0-7524-0139-4

Horsforth
Alan Cockroft and Matthew Young
ISBN 0-7524-0130-0

Knaresborough
Arnold Kellett
ISBN 0-7524-0131-9

Around Leeds
Matthew Young and Dorothy Payne
ISBN 0-7524-0168-8

Penistone
Matthew Young and David Hambleton
ISBN 0-7524-0138-6

Selby from the William Rawling Collection
Matthew Young
ISBN 0-7524-0198-X

Central Sheffield
Martin Olive
ISBN 0-7524-0011-8

Around Stocksbridge
Stocksbridge and District History Society
ISBN 0-7524-0165-3

TRANSPORT

Filton and the Flying Machine
Malcolm Hall
ISBN 0-7524-0171-8

Gloster Aircraft Company
Derek James
ISBN 0-7524-0038-X

Great Western Swindon
Tim Bryan
ISBN 0-7524-0153-X

Midland and South Western Junction Railway
Mike Barnsley and Brian Bridgeman
ISBN 0-7524-0016-9

Shorts Aircraft
Mike Hooks
ISBN 0-7524-0193-9

This stock list shows all titles available in the United Kingdom as at 30 September 1995.

ORDER FORM

The books in this stock list are available from your local bookshop. Alternatively they are available by mail order at a totally inclusive price of £10.00 per copy.

For overseas orders please add the following postage supplement for each copy ordered:
European Union £0.36 (this includes the Republic of Ireland)
Royal Mail Zone 1 (for example, U.S.A. and Canada) £1.96
Royal Mail Zone 2 (for example, Australia and New Zealand) £2.47

Please note that all of these supplements are actual Royal Mail charges with no profit element to the Chalford Publishing Company. Furthermore, as the Air Mail Printed Papers rate applies, we are restricted from enclosing any personal correspondence other than to indicate the senders name.

Payment can be made by cheque, Visa or Mastercard. Please indicate your method of payment on this order form.

If you are not entirely happy with your purchase you may return it within 30 days of receipt for a full refund.

Please send your order to:

The Chalford Publishing Company,
St Mary's Mill,
Chalford,
Stroud,
Gloucestershire
GL6 8NX

This order form should perforate away from the book. However, if you are reluctant to damage the book in any way we are quite happy to accept a photocopy order form or a letter containing the necessary information.

PLEASE WRITE CLEARLY USING BLOCK CAPITALS

Name and address of the person ordering the books listed below:

_____

_____

_____ Post code _____

Please also supply your telephone number in case we have difficulty fully understanding your requirements. Tel.: _____ - _____

Name and address of where the books are to be despatched to (if different from above):

_____

_____

_____ Post code _____

Please indicate here if you would like to receive future information on books published by the Chalford Publishing Company.

____ Yes, please put me on your mailing list   ____ No, please just send the books ordered below

Title	ISBN	Quantity
....	0-7524-_____-___	_____
....	0-7524-_____-___	_____
....	0-7524-_____-___	_____
....	0-7524-_____-___	_____
....	0-7524-_____-___	_____
	Total number of books	_____

Cost of books delivered in UK = Number of books ordered @ £10 each =£ _____

Overseas postage supplement (if relevant)   =£ _____

TOTAL PAYMENT   =£ _____

Method of Payment   ❑ Cheque   ❑ Visa   ❑ Mastercard   **VISA**

Please make cheques payable to *The Chalford Publishing Company*   MasterCard

Name of Card Holder _____

Card Number ❑❑❑❑❑❑❑❑❑❑❑❑❑❑❑❑❑❑❑

Expiry date ❑❑ / ❑❑

I authorise payment of £_____ from the above card

Signed _____